THE MAKING OF THE MODERN WORLD
1945 TO THE PRESENT

Women, Minorities, and Changing Social Structures

BOOKS IN THE SERIES

Culture and Customs in a Connected World

Education, Poverty, and Inequality

Food, Population, and the Environment

Governance and the Quest for Security

Health and Medicine

Migration and Refugees

Science and Technology

Trade, Economic Life, and Globalization

Women, Minorities, and Changing Social Structures

THE MAKING OF THE MODERN WORLD

1945 TO THE PRESENT

Women, Minorities, and Changing Social Structures

John Perritano

SERIES ADVISOR
Ruud van Dijk

Mason Crest

Mason Crest
450 Parkway Drive, Suite D
Broomall, PA 19008
www.masoncrest.com

Produced and developed by MTM Publishing.
www.mtmpublishing.com

President: Valerie Tomaselli
Designer: Sherry Williams, Oxygen Design Group
Copyeditor: Lee Motteler, GeoMap Corp.
Editorial Coordinator: Andrea St. Aubin
Proofreader: Peter Jaskowiak

ISBN: 978-1-4222-3643-7
Series ISBN: 978-1-4222-3634-5
Ebook ISBN: 978-1-4222-8287-8

Library of Congress Cataloging-in-Publication Data

Names: Perritano, John, author.
Title: Women, minorities, and changing social structures / by John Perritano.
Description: Broomall, PA : Mason Crest, 2016. | Series: Making of the modern world: 1945 to the present | Includes index.
Identifiers: LCCN 2016020059| ISBN 9781422236437 (hardback) | ISBN 9781422236345 (series) | ISBN 9781422282878 (ebook)
Subjects: LCSH: Women. | Women and war. | Minorities--Social conditions. | Multiculturalism. | Social structure. | Globalization--Social aspects.
Classification: LCC HQ1206 .P4267 2016 | DDC 305.4--dc23
LC record available at https://lccn.loc.gov/2016020059

Printed and bound in the United States of America.

First printing
9 8 7 6 5 4 3 2 1

Contents

KEY ICONS TO LOOK FOR:

Words to understand: These words with their easy-to-understand definitions will increase the reader's understanding of the text while building vocabulary skills.

Sidebars: This boxed material within the main text allows readers to build knowledge, gain insights, explore possibilities, and broaden their perspectives by weaving together additional information to provide realistic and holistic perspectives.

Educational Videos: Readers can view videos by scanning our QR codes, providing them with additional educational content to supplement the text. Examples include news coverage, moments in history, speeches, iconic sports moments and much more!

Text-dependent questions: These questions send the reader back to the text for more careful attention to the evidence presented there.

Research projects: Readers are pointed toward areas of further inquiry connected to each chapter. Suggestions are provided for projects that encourage deeper research and analysis.

Series Introduction

In 1945, at the end of World War II, the world had to start afresh in many ways. The war had affected the entire world, destroying cities, sometimes entire regions, and killing millions. At the end of the war, millions more were displaced or on the move, while hunger, disease, and poverty threatened survivors everywhere the war had been fought.

Politically, the old, European-dominated order had been discredited. Western European democracies had failed to stop Hitler, and in Asia they had been powerless against imperial Japan. The autocratic, militaristic Axis powers had been defeated. But their victory was achieved primarily through the efforts of the Soviet Union—a communist dictatorship—and the United States, which was the only democracy powerful enough to aid Great Britain and the other Allied powers in defeating the Axis onslaught. With the European colonial powers weakened, the populations of their respective empires now demanded their independence.

The war had truly been a global catastrophe. It underlined the extent to which peoples and countries around the world were interconnected and interdependent. However, the search for shared approaches to major, global challenges in the postwar world—symbolized by the founding of the United Nations—was soon overshadowed by the Cold War. The leading powers in this contest, the United States and the Soviet Union, represented mutually exclusive visions for the postwar world. The Soviet Union advocated collectivism, centrally planned economies, and a leading role for the Communist Party. The United States sought to promote liberal democracy, symbolized by free markets and open political systems. Each believed fervently in the promise and justice of its vision for the future. And neither thought it could compromise on what it considered vital interests. Both were concerned about whose influence would dominate Europe, for example, and to whom newly independent nations in the non-Western world would pledge their allegiance. As a result, the postwar world would be far from peaceful.

As the Cold War proceeded, peoples living beyond the Western world and outside the control of the Soviet Union began to find their voices. Driven by decolonization, the developing world, or so-called Third World, took on a new importance. In particular, countries in these areas were potential allies on both sides of the Cold War. As the newly independent peoples established their own identities and built viable states, they resisted the sometimes coercive pull of the Cold War superpowers, while also trying to use them for their own ends. In addition, a new Communist China, established in 1949 and the largest country in the developing world, was deeply entangled within the Cold War contest between communist and capitalist camps. Over the coming decades, however, it would come to act ever more independently from either the United States or the Soviet Union.

During the war, governments had made significant strides in developing new technologies in areas such as aviation, radar, missile technology, and, most ominous, nuclear energy. Scientific and technological breakthroughs achieved in a military context held promise for civilian applications, and thus were poised to contribute to recovery and, ultimately, prosperity. In other fields, it also seemed time for a fresh start. For example, education could be used to "re-educate" members of aggressor nations and further Cold War agendas, but education could also help more people take advantage of, and contribute to, the possibilities of the new age of science and technology.

For several decades after 1945, the Cold War competition seemed to dominate, and indeed define, the postwar world. Driven by ideology, the conflict extended into politics, economics, science and technology, and culture. Geographically, it came to affect virtually the entire world. From our twenty-first-century vantage point, however, it is clear that well before the Cold War's end in the late 1980s, the world had been moving on from the East-West conflict.

Looking back, it appears that, despite divisions—between communist and capitalist camps, or between developed and developing countries—the world after 1945 was growing more and more interconnected. After the Cold War, this increasingly came to be called "globalization." People in many different places faced shared challenges. And as time went on, an awareness of this interconnectedness grew. One response by people in and outside of governments was to seek common approaches, to think and act globally. Another was to protect national, local, or private autonomy, to keep the outside world at bay. Neither usually existed by itself; reality was generally some combination of the two.

Thematically organized, the nine volumes in this series explore how the post-World War II world gradually evolved from the fractured ruins of 1945, through the various crises of the Cold War and the decolonization process, to a world characterized by interconnectedness and interdependence. The accounts in these volumes reinforce each other, and are best studied together. Taking them as a whole will build a broad understanding of the ways in which "globalization" has become the defining feature of the world in the early twenty-first century.

However, the volumes are designed to stand on their own. Tracing the evolution of trade and the global economy, for example, the reader will learn enough about the political context to get a broader understanding of the times. Of course, studying economic developments will likely lead to curiosity about scientific and technological progress, social and cultural change, poverty and education, and more. In other words, studying one volume should lead to interest in the others. In the end, no element of our globalizing world can be fully understood in isolation.

The volumes do not have to be read in a specific order. It is best to be led by one's own interests in deciding where to start. What we recommend is a curious, critical stance throughout the study of the world's history since World War II: to keep asking questions about the causes of events, to keep looking for connections to deepen your understanding of how we have gotten to where we are today. If students achieve this goal with the help of our volumes, we—and they—will have succeeded.

—Ruud van Dijk

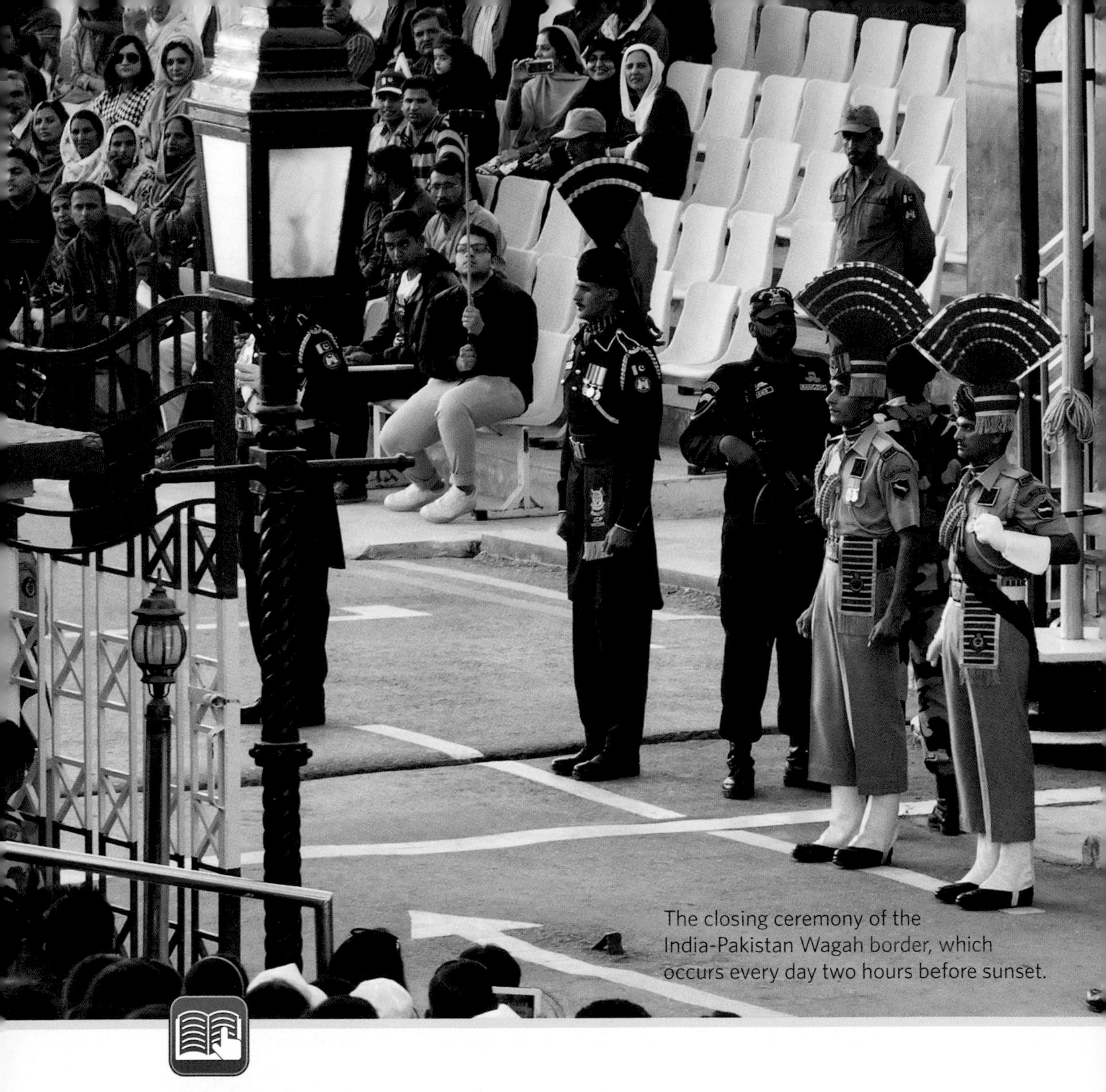

The closing ceremony of the India-Pakistan Wagah border, which occurs every day two hours before sunset.

WORDS TO UNDERSTAND

aberration: departure from what is normal.

genocide: systematic killing of the members of a particular political, racial, or ethnic group.

indigenous: native to a region or country.

nationalistic: relating to devotion to a nation and national identity.

subcontinent: here, the region in South Asia occupied now by Bangladesh, India, and Pakistan.

CHAPTER

1

War and Its Aftermath

The sun was setting on the British Empire when World War II ended in 1945. Although Britain helped defeat Nazi Germany and its allies, the colonial superpower had emerged from the war badly bruised and in economic tatters. Pushed along by **nationalistic** movements across the empire, Britain's new Labour government decided to abandon many of its overseas colonies, including India, one of its most prized possessions. The idea was to form two separate nations on the **subcontinent**. The first, India, would be dominated by its Hindu majority. The second, Pakistan, would be dominated by Muslims. For as far back as anyone could remember, the Hindus, Muslims, and Sikhs, a minority religion in India, were somewhat tolerant of one another when the British were in charge. All that ended in 1947 as independence uprooted some 12 million people. Hindus, now a minority in Pakistan, were forced to move into India, while Muslims, now a minority in India, were forced to move to Pakistan. In the process, an undeclared civil war broke out as long-simmering hostilities over culture, economics, religion, territory, and politics boiled to the surface. About 1 million people were murdered. Many others died of disease and malnutrition. Both sides committed unspeakable atrocities, including the raping of women.

Yet, the persecution of minorities during the postwar era was not an **aberration** confined to just India and Pakistan. The old colonial powers of Europe no longer held sway when World War II ended. Many found it difficult and expensive to maintain their colonies in Asia, Africa, and the Middle East. Consequently, the Europeans were forced to abandon their overseas territories. Some, like Britain, did so grudgingly but voluntarily. Others, such as Belgium, France, and the Netherlands, were more reluctant. Independence in many colonies came only after wars of national liberation.

Many of these new nations now found themselves in the middle of an ethnic, religious, cultural, and economic maelstrom as various groups began to "rediscover" their cultural identities free from colonial shackles. Consequently, internal animosities threw many fledging nations into chaos. Grievances over economic inequality, lack of democracy, civil liberties, and state-sponsored discrimination against mi-

Prisoners in a Nazi concentration camp at Ebensee, Austria, when they were liberated by the U.S. Army in 1945.

nority religions, women, and others produced instability, poverty, and civil conflict.

In Europe itself, the immediate aftermath of the war played out in further ethnic conflicts. The war bred animosities that were carried over into postwar Europe. For instance, ethnic Germans fled or were evicted from many areas in Eastern and Central Europe in the massive population transfers at the end of the war.

Human Rights

Human rights were at the center of many of these conflicts. Since the end of World War II, the international community has tried to find ways to implement policies that would address grievances of minority groups that had suffered. Specifically, the United Nations, formed when the war ended, took the lead in protecting the rights of minorities.

Abusing the rights of humans, especially those belonging to minority groups, was not new in world history. However, World War II brought the issue to the forefront in a new way. During the war, the Nazis in Germany exterminated more than 6 million Jews, Roma (gypsies), homosexuals, and persons with mental and physical disabilities, an atrocity now known as the Holocaust. The Nazis committed this **genocide** as part of their goal of racial purity. Germany's allies, especially Japan, also abused ethnic and religious groups in the nations they conquered. The Japanese conducted scientific experiments on Chinese civilians, while turning many Korean women into sexual slaves. The Japanese also committed a range of atrocities against **indigenous** groups in South Asia and against Chinese Muslims. Even the United States, which participated in the war to stop the aggressors, committed human rights abuses: it set up internment camps for Japanese Americans because the government feared that they might be a security threat.

When the war ended with the defeat of Germany and Japan, the victorious Allied nations, led by the United States, France, Great Britain, the Soviet Union, and others, formed the United Nations. Its goal was to ensure peace in the postwar world and to help guard against future human rights abuses, including such massive occurrences as the Nazi genocide. To that end, the UN hashed out a set of standards that would hold governments accountable for how they treated their citizens.

Although the organization's charter contained references to human rights, many believed that something more substantial was needed—a universal declaration of rights. The main world powers, especially the Soviet Union, the United States, and Great Britain, at first balked at drawing up such a document. Nevertheless, the General Assembly created the UN Commission on Human Rights and appointed Eleanor Roosevelt, the widow of U.S. President Franklin Roosevelt, as its first chairperson.

The job of creating a human rights document for the world proved a bit frustrating for the strong-willed former first lady. Roosevelt found herself in the center of one of the first Cold War disputes with the Soviets. She saw firsthand that the Soviet definitions of "free-

OTHER TREATIES

The Universal Declaration of Human Rights led to other international treaties, including the International Covenant on Civil and Political Rights and the International Covenant on Economic, Social and Cultural Rights. Ratified by the UN General Assembly in 1966, these treaties each went a bit further than the UDHR in clearly outlining how the international community should think about the rights of all humans.

Eleanor Roosevelt, the first chairperson for the UN Commission on Human Rights, led the efforts to craft and pass the Universal Declaration of Human Rights in 1948.

IN THEIR OWN WORDS

Eleanor Roosevelt, Chairperson of the UN Commission on Human Rights

Where, after all, do universal human rights begin? In small places, close to home—so close and so small that they cannot be seen on any maps of the world. Yet they are the world of the individual person; the neighborhood he lives in; the school or college he attends; the factory, farm, or office where he works. Such are the places where every man, woman, and child seeks equal justice, equal opportunity, equal dignity without discrimination.

– From a 1958 speech to the United Nations marking the tenth anniversary of the Universal Declaration of Human Rights.

dom" and "democracy" were not quite the same as the American definitions. The Soviets wanted to make sure each country decided whether a specific human right had been violated, as opposed to allowing other countries or an international body to make that decision. The Soviets also wanted to make sure that employment, education, and health care were included as basic human rights. In the view of the Soviets, these rights were just as important as political rights.

Negotiations were long, arduous, and tense. The Soviets proved difficult at nearly every turn and blasted the United States for its institutional racial discrimination against African Americans. In the end, compromises were reached, and the Universal Declaration of Human Rights (UDHR) was adopted by the UN in 1948.

The UDHR was intended to guide the actions of the United Nations and its member countries, providing an outline of basic human rights. Although it was not legally binding, the declaration was historic nonetheless, even though it lacked specifics such as recognizing minority rights.

"All human beings are born free and equal in dignity and rights," Article 1 began. "They are endowed with reason and conscience and should act toward one another in a spirit of brotherhood." The UDHR then outlined various rights, including rights to life, liberty, and property. People should not be arrested without just cause or be tortured as they had been during World War II. People had the right to think freely and express themselves. Religious freedom was also a basic right.

The document was idealistic, yet many nations embraced its goals. Its principles would guide other UN agencies as they worked to protect workers, women, children, and refugees. Countries invoked its language to protest racism and colonialism. At the same time, human rights abuses against minorities and women continued through the decades following. Enforcing human rights was often very difficult: it usually took a multination effort, as many countries resisted the very idea of an outside entity having a say in their internal affairs.

Text-Dependent Questions

1. When was the Indian subcontinent partitioned into the states of India and Pakistan?
2. When was the Universal Declaration of Human Rights adopted by the United Nations?
3. Who was the first chairperson of the UN Commission on Human Rights?

Research Projects

1. Use the Internet and the library to write a detailed report on the Universal Declaration of Human Rights.
2. Create a timeline of the various political, ethnic, and religious conflicts between India and Pakistan since each country's independence.

Educational Video

Eleanor Roosevelt Speech on Human Rights
Page 11–12

Archival footage from the FDR Presidential Library of a speech recorded by Eleanor Roosevelt for a television program on Human Rights Day.

Published on YouTube by PublicResourceOrg. https://youtu.be/sPVWmmVKVk0.

WORDS TO UNDERSTAND

bifurcated: divided in two.

consumerism: belief that personal consumption of material goods is a sign of economic health and strength.

feminism: political and social movement committed to expanding and securing women's rights.

manifesto: declaration of principles.

oral contraceptive: birth control pill.

ABOVE: U.S. vice president Richard Nixon and Soviet premier Nikita Khrushchev during the Kitchen Debate.

CHAPTER

2

Women in the Postwar World

In the summer of 1959, Richard Nixon, vice president of the United States, traveled to the Soviet Union to attend the opening of the American National Exhibition in Moscow. At the time, the Americans and Soviets were locked in the Cold War—a bitter clash of ideologies as each tried to spread its own economic and social philosophies around the world. At the exhibition, Nixon and Soviet premier Nikita Khrushchev debated the merits of communism versus democracy. As they stood in the exhibit of a modern kitchen, the two heatedly argued about peace, **consumerism**, nuclear weapons, and industry, as well as the role of women in each society.

"In America, we like to make life easier for women," Nixon boasted.

"Your capitalist attitude toward women does not occur under communism," Khrushchev shot back.

"I think that this attitude towards women is universal," Nixon answered. "What we want to do is make life more easy for our housewives."

Dissecting the so-called Kitchen Debate years later, historian Helen Laville said despite the social, economic, and philosophical differences between the two societies, one concept between the two rang true: "Civilized and advanced societies were those which relieved women of the burden of work; uncivilized and backwards societies were those which extract hard labor from their women."

Most women's daily lives revolved around housework, even though many stepped into the workforce during World War II as men left for the front lines.

War Changes Everything

The prevailing view of women prior to World War II was that of homemaker, mother, and housewife. When war came, new opportunities emerged as women became deeply woven into the economic fabric of life. As men marched off to combat, women in a number of nations were not only asked to keep the home fires burning, but also to keep the factories running. They worked building ships, tanks, guns, and other war-related products. Women also took over other male-dominated jobs, including taxi drivers, railroad workers, and streetcar conductors. In the United States, women occupied jobs in almost every part of the U.S. economy. Females in the labor force, according to the *Encyclopedia of U.S. Labor and Working-Class History*, increased by more than 6 million between 1940 and 1945.

Women were also pressed into service in Japan, one of the war's Axis powers. Prior to the war, women made up a significant percentage of workers in Japan's textile industry. Once they got married, however, women were expected to leave their jobs and tend to their families. The war changed all that. At first, the Japanese government did not encourage women to work in factories. By 1943, however, Japan was losing its male population as war casualties were mounting. The government asked all unmarried women and those fifteen years old or older to work in Japan's factories. By 1944, more than 4 million Japanese women were working building airplanes and bombs. They also worked in other fields.

Four U.S. women trained to fly the B-17 Flying Fortress as part of the Women Airforce Service Pilots (WASP). From left to right, Frances Green, Margaret (Peg) Kirchner, Ann Waldner, and Blanche Osborn.

Captain Mariya Dolina, a pilot for the Soviet forces during World War II who commanded a dive bomber squadron. In 1945 she was honored as a "Hero of the Soviet Union" for her service during the war.

In the Soviet Union, women also played an important and decisive role during the war, as they worked in a number of industries and served in the military. Although many American and British women served with the armed forces, they generally took supporting roles. In the Soviet Union, however, women were on the front lines as machine gunners, snipers, and members of tank crews.

After the War

When the war ended, life for women changed drastically: they lost most of the social and economic independence they enjoyed during the war. As the men returned home, most women went back to their traditional roles as homemakers. In the United States, women who wanted to continue in their jobs were often laid off as veterans returned and settled into the labor force. Younger women, who were still in school during the war, suffered the most as they reached working age. They competed for jobs with returning soldiers and older women who remained in the labor market. Many young women who were locked out of the job market resigned themselves to marriage and having children.

The result was a "baby boom" that helped return postwar women to their conventional prewar roles. More than 3.4 million babies were born in the United States a year after the war ended, according to "Baby Boomers" at History.com; more than 4 million children were born annually from 1954 until 1964, when the number of births leveled off. At that point, 76.4 million "baby boomers" had been born in the United States.

The situation played itself out in other countries, too. In Canada, for example, 400,000 babies were born each year from 1952 to 1966, according to data reported in Jennie Bristow's *Baby Boomers and Generational Conflict*. Births also skyrocketed in Europe, including in France, the United Kingdom, Germany, and Finland. The

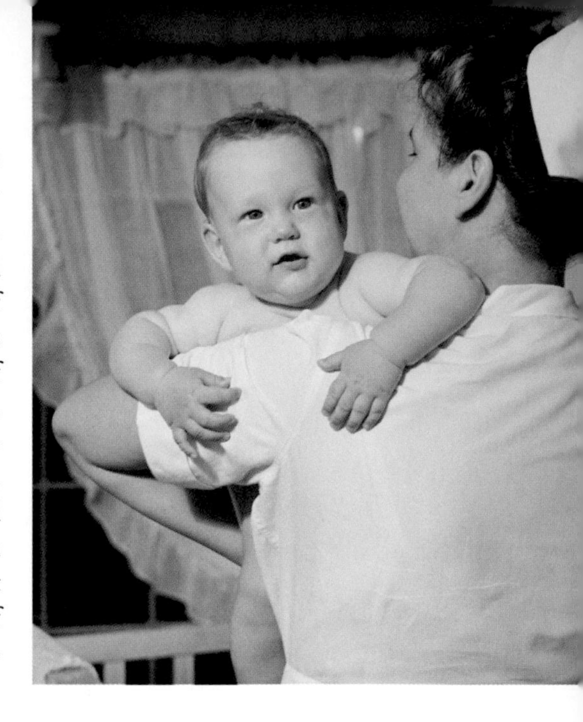

A baby boom occurred in many Western countries following World War II.

increased birthrate changed society. Suburbs sprang up outside cities as a need for living space increased. A new era of consumerism dawned in the West as new products were produced, many of which were aimed at the homemaker. The number of shopping centers, supermarkets, and fast-food restaurants grew. More pointedly, the baby boom helped to sharpen the traditional roles between wife and husband, mother and father. It solidified the man as the breadwinner of the house and the wife as its chief domestic caretaker.

Aftermath in Japan and Russia

The war left Japan in ruins and the Allies as occupiers. Consequently, the United States began to remold Japanese society using democratic values and institutions. Japanese women suddenly found that they had many of the same rights as women in Western societies. Japanese women now could vote and had the opportunity to go to school. Yet these new cultural standards did not mean total equality for Japanese women. Women workers still earned less than men did, and many women lacked a proper education.

In the communist Soviet Union, women were theoretically equal to men in all aspects of life. While universal equality is the overriding principle of communism, it was not the dominant practice. Soviet women, as they were in many societies, were still treated as second-class citizens. Their roles varied by social status and where they lived. Rural peasants were the lowest class in the Soviet Union's supposedly classless society. While the Soviet system instituted legal equality between the sexes, rural women were in fact at a disadvantage. Husbands worked in the fields, and women were responsible for both the home and family, likely after they worked in the field. In cities, state-run factories preferred men to women.

The woman's role in the postwar Soviet Union was **bifurcated**, to say the least. Women were asked not only to help rebuild the country's shattered economy, but also to repopulate the nation. Most, in the immediate aftermath of the war at least, decided to focus their attention on their households rather than bolstering the Soviet economic system.

Women in China

For centuries, women in China were looked on as possessions, first by their birth families, and later by their husbands. They did not have political rights and were forced to obey the males in their lives. During the 1949 communist revolution, however, China's new leader, Mao Zedong, enacted a series of reforms that reshaped the role of women in Chinese society. One of his reforms, the Marriage Reform Law, for example, stipulated that "all marriages are to be based on the free consent of men and women." Under Mao, it became easier for wives to divorce husbands, which was nearly impossible a few years before.

Mao also banned the killing of female babies and the forced sale of women into prostitution. Arranged marriages were done away with, as was the practice of binding women's feet, a status symbol among the elite and a way for families with daughters to achieve upward mobility.

"Women hold up half the sky," Mao intoned, and he quickly made sure they were paid the same as men, had access to the same education, and could own property, just as men could. Women became doctors, engineers, political party operatives, and scientists. Yet equality came with a price. While women labored outside the house on an equal basis with men, they still had to rear children, cook meals, clean, and sew. Moreover, government urged women (and men) to have more babies, reasoning that more children meant more workers and ultimately a stronger economy. The plan failed miserably, as China's population grew so quickly that it outstripped the government's ability to feed, educate, and house its citizens.

Although Mao's disastrous Great Leap Forward, in which he sought to replace China's old customs and ideas with new socialist practices, was unsuccessful, his campaign to get women to work outside the home showed promise. Under Deng Xiaoping, who became Mao's successor in 1978 and led the country until 1989, women's status improved greatly. Chinese women now have more educational and business opportunities. Although China's government is still dominated by men, women have made stunning advances in the private sector. Six of the top fourteen women on *Forbes* magazine's list of female billionaires in 2015 were Chinese.

Two Chinese women at a factory for making tools in 1956.

IN THEIR OWN WORDS

Mao Zedong, Communist Leader of China

In order to build a great socialist society it is of the utmost importance to arouse the broad masses of women to join in productive activity. Men and women must receive equal pay for equal work in production. Genuine equality between the sexes can only be realized in the process of the socialist transformation of society as a whole.

–From Mao's "Women Have Gone to the Labour Front" (1955).

The Ever-Changing Role of Women

"The problem lay buried, unspoken, for many years in the minds of American women. It was a strange stirring, a sense of dissatisfaction, a yearning that women suffered in the middle of the twentieth century. . . . Each suburban wife struggled with it alone. As she made the beds, shopped for groceries . . . lay beside her husband at night—she was afraid to ask even of herself the silent question—'Is this all?'"

So begins the first chapter in Betty Friedan's 1963 book, *The Feminine Mystique* which many credit with launching modern **feminism**. Although it was not a political **manifesto** the book took a critical and eye-opening look at women's lives in the postwar United States. Friedan, a suburban housewife and freelance writer, called on women to look beyond the role of homemaker and to throw off the shackles that bound them to house, children, and husband.

As the 1960s dawned, many Western women took a hard look at their lives, and many decided that they wanted more as economies grew and nations prospered. From the United States to Great Britain, from France to West Germany and beyond, the "women's liberation" movement fought for equal pay, equal rights at work, reproductive rights, and laws against sexual harassment.

It was a liberating time for women. They joined the workforce in record numbers, even though their wages lagged far behind those of men. The introduction of the birth control pill, an **oral contraceptive**, in 1960 meant that women could now control their own sexuality and determine when they were ready to have children.

It wasn't just women in the West who were changing. Laws in many countries made it easier for husbands and wives to get divorced. In many cases, women now had the right to vote. In addition, more women, such as Sirimavo Bandaranaike in Sri Lanka, Indira Gandhi in India, and Golda Meir in Israel, broke the male-dominated ceiling of twentieth-century politics to become leaders of nations.

Indira Gandhi, prime minister of India from 1966 to 1977, and then again from 1980 until she was assassinated in 1984.

Betty Friedan, author of *The Feminine Mystique.*

Disparities Continued

As Western women slowly made gains, women living in the Middle East and sub-Saharan Africa lagged behind. Many colonial governments, such as those in the British colonies of Rhodesia and Kenya, barred rural women from cities, expecting them to farm and help rear children. Many of these women protested by boycotting businesses, leading workers' strikes, and holding other demonstrations. They became politically active, and once independence was achieved many fought to attain equal rights with men.

Across Africa and the Middle East, these rights were granted in many cases; however, male heads of households and tribal leaders still made decisions. This disparity often led to financial problems and unequal access to education, income, and property. Girls in sub-Saharan Africa, for example, were more than likely to drop out of school than boys. Poor families tended to spend whatever money they had on the education of boys, because males were considered future breadwinners. Girls were expected to carry on traditional domestic work and marry young.

Compared to men, women in Africa and in other developing regions were not allowed to make decisions, limiting their financial and social mobility. The poorest countries were often wracked by violence and natural disasters, resulting in greater gender inequalities.

The disparities continue today. According to the International Center for Research on Women, 33 percent of girls are forced to marry before turning eighteen, while 11 percent are forced into marriages by the age of fifteen. The number is much higher in specific countries, such as Nigeria, where 75 percent of girls marry before they turn eighteen, and in Chad, where 65 percent of the girls marry. The consequences are grave, as girls suffer from high infant mortality rates, higher maternal mortality rates, and lower education.

STRICT INTERPRETATIONS OF ISLAM

Strict interpretations of Islamic law have made women targets of violence in recent years. According to the United Nations, in Morocco, sexual violence affects 40 percent of eighteen- to twenty-four-year-old women. In other countries, rape and forced marriage are commonplace. As part of an extreme version of Islamic law, called Sharia, women are often stoned and publically whipped for engaging in sex outside marriage.

Women in the Islamic World

While it is true that Muslim women have struggled against inequality for centuries, it is more from local cultural traditions than any teachings in the Koran. According to the Koran, women have a right to choose their husbands. They can inherit wealth and control their own money and property.

Nevertheless, the role of women in Muslim society has been varied as social, political, and economic circumstances shifted. Over the centuries, males have not treated Muslim women as their equals. Since the beginning of the Cold War, women have been caught between traditionalists and reformers as Islamic societies have become independent nations. Men have used their interpretation of Muslim law to decide how women should live their daily lives. Although there are examples of Muslim women who have been important in public life, Muslim women are looked upon mostly as wives, homemakers, and mothers. Additionally, a man can have more than one wife.

In some Muslim societies, such as Saudi Arabia, a woman is allowed to work, go to school, and travel only with the written permission of a male guardian. A woman must always obey her husband. Scripture also permits men to divorce their wives without cause. However, divorce is not all one-sided: the pair can seek an arbitrator's help in reconciling, and women have the power to initiate a divorce proceeding as well. If the breakup is not the husband's fault, the woman must return her dowry to dissolve the marriage. If the husband is at fault, he must pay back the dowry.

Many Muslim women activists have tried to draw attention to and do away with discriminatory laws and male-centered practices that permeate many Muslim societies. The ascent of radical Islamic ideology has made their work extremely difficult.

A Muslim woman in 2015 protesting on Women's Day in Kolkata, India.

Text-Dependent Questions

1. During which years did the "baby boom" occur?
2. In which year was the communist revolution in China?
3. Who wrote *The Feminine Mystique*?

Research Projects

1. Interview a grandmother, an aunt, or another woman who remembers what it was like being a woman in the 1950s and 1960s. Next, interview another woman who remembers what it was like being a woman in the 1970s and 1980s. Ask questions about the challenges each faced. Compare the two. Are there any similarities? What were the differences? What conclusions can you draw?
2. Research the role of Soviet women in World War II. Present an oral report on what you discovered.

Biafrans, a minority Nigerian ethnic group, marching in a May Day rally in Athens, Greece, their adopted country.

WORDS TO UNDERSTAND

autonomy: self-government.

conglomerations: collections of individuals, entities, or groups, often unrelated to each other.

regime: group ruling and administering the government of a country.

sanctions: policies or tools used against a government or other entity to influence their actions.

segregation: policy of separating individuals or a group from the majority of a population.

separatists: those seeking independence or autonomy for their region within a country.

CHAPTER

3

Ethnic Minorities in the Postwar World

As dozens of new nations materialized from the chaos of World War II—created out of nationalistic movements or out of international mandates—a new set of conflicts emerged, rooted in long-simmering ethnic and religious animosities. From Sri Lanka to Yugoslavia, from South Africa to Northern Ireland, ethnoreligious tensions created what some historians have called unrestrained "global chaos."

After the war, many national borders were drawn without considering racial, ethnic, or regional differences. Many nations became **conglomerations** of culturally diverse populations made up of groups that had deep-seeded hatred of one another. While many ethnic minorities were able to live alongside each other peaceably, others were not. In many cases, minorities controlled the government and imposed their will on the majority, such as the white Afrikaners over the black majority in South Africa. In other cases, ethnic majorities dominated and used their power to oppress minority groups.

Such ethnic conflicts usually simmered under the surface of stable societies. In many instances, the governing class was unaware or did not want to recognize that these tensions existed. In some cases, such as the struggle of French Canadians seeking **autonomy** in Quebec, the conflict was generally nonviolent. In other nations, tensions exploded in genocidal murder. Ethnic struggles often unleashed a refugee crisis and unspeakable human rights' violations.

Ethnic Tensions Brewing in the Soviet Union and Europe

The Soviet Union and Soviet Bloc countries were home to many ethnic conflicts—most with deep historical roots, emerging into full-blown conflicts during the Soviet rule, and some after communism fell. Implied in its full official name, the Union of Soviet Socialist Republics incorporated many independent regions and distinct ethnic groups under one nation when it was created in 1918; in fact, many had been

GROUPS WITHIN GROUPS

Every society is made up of ethnic groups. Sociologists have divided these groups into five subsets, each with different political agendas. They include the following:

- ***ethnonationalists*** who want their ethnic community to have absolute authority over their own political, economic, and social affairs
- ***communal contenders*** whose goal is to share power, rather than fight for autonomy
- ***indigenous people*** descended from the original inhabitants of a region who often defend their way of life against systematic encroachment
- ***ethnoclasses*** that are distinct minorities, such as Koreans in Japan and people of color in North America; while members of an ethnoclass often benefit economically, they have little or no political power
- ***militant sects*** that are religiously politicized minorities dominated by other religious traditions, such as Muslim Arabs in Israel and Sikhs in India

part of the Russian Empire prior to the creation of the Soviet Union. In oil-rich Azerbaijan, for example, the Azeris, a Turkic ethnic group, were the majority. However, in the region of Nagorno-Karabakh, ethnic Armenians outnumbered the Azeris. Conflict between Azeris and Armenians in Azerbaijan became pronounced in the early years of the Soviet Union. As the Soviet Union disintegrated, Nagorno-Karabakh declared independence from Azerbaijan and an ethnic war ensued. A cease-fire was reached in 1994, although violence still occurred.

With the collapse of communism in the early 1990s, other ethnic tensions flared. In 1994, **separatists** in Chechnya, home to many ethnic and religious groups, including Muslim Chechens, tried to break away from Russian rule. The Russians responded by crushing the rebellion. In the process, tens of thousands of civilians were killed as both sides committed atrocities, including a Chechen terrorist attack that killed schoolchildren in the city of Beslan.

The situation in Yugoslavia was bloodier and more complicated. Like the Soviet Union, Yugoslavia was a multiethnic communist state that included people in the republics of Serbia, Croatia, Montenegro, Slovenia, Macedonia, Kosovo, and Bosnia and Herzegovina. The majority of Yugoslavians all spoke the same language, but each republic was dominated by one ethnic group. Nationally, the Serbs controlled the Yugoslav government, which was held together by Josip Broz Tito, longtime communist leader.

Chechen fighters near the Presidential Palace in the Chechen capital of Grozny, praying in front of an eternal flame in 1994.

Gravediggers working to bury the dead in Sarajevo, Bosnia, during the ethnic violence there.

Tito died in 1980, and communism collapsed a decade later; by then, nationalistic unrest had spread throughout the region. The Serbs wanted to preserve the Yugoslavian state, but Slovenia and Croatia each declared independence in 1991. That move triggered a war between Serbs and Croats. Other republics soon broke away, tossing the entire region into turmoil. In 1992, as many countries recognized the independence of Croatia and Slovenia, Bosnia and Herzegovina declared its independence. In response, the Serbian army launched attacks against Bosnian Muslims, who had voted for Bosnian independence.

Although many countries recognized Bosnia as an independent state, Bosnian Serbs attacked Sarajevo, the capital of Bosnia and Herzegovina, in 1992, with support from the Serbian republic. At first people thought that 200,000 people died in Bosnia during the next nineteen months. That figure has since been reduced to 100,000. Eighty-two percent of the civilians killed in the war were Muslim; 10 percent were Serbs. After several European Union (EU) and UN initiatives failed to stop the fighting, the use of North Atlantic Treaty Organization (NATO) forces, along with U.S.-led diplomacy, resulted in the so-called Dayton Accords in 1995.

In 1998, Kosovo also experienced similar strife. Ethnic Albanians accounted for about 90 percent of Kosovo's population; the remaining portion were Serbian. With its autonomy increasingly squeezed by Belgrade, the larger group resisted Serb influence, but in response, the Yugoslav army attacked ethnic Albanians living in the region. Eventually, the nineteen nations of NATO stepped in, bombing Yugoslavia's military and forcing Serbian troops from Kosovo.

Peace eventually settled over the region, and the various groups came to various accommodations in order to reconcile their differences and forsake armed conflict. In Bosnia and Herzegovina, as well as Kosovo, compromise was the route to peace. International pressure and diplomacy—including from the EU, NATO, the United States, and the United Nations—all played a role, some more effective than others. The prospect of membership in the EU and NATO, another tool of international pressure, also offered incentives to the warring factions to put down their arms.

THE IMPACT OF APARTHEID

For decades, apartheid controlled the lives of blacks, as the white minority ruled South Africa with a racist hand. Whites made up less than one-fifth of the country's population, but they passed racist laws and controlled the country's best land and economic resources. All nonwhites, for example, had to get legal permits to travel within the country, which they had to carry with them at all times.

Blacks resisted apartheid through the African National Congress, led by Nelson Mandela. In the 1980s, after much violence and massive international pressure that included economic **sanctions**, South Africa began to democratize. In 1994, South Africans of every race were able to vote for the first time. They elected Mandela president.

Ethnic Conflicts in Africa

Ethnic conflicts also played out with increasing regularity in Africa. National unity during Africa's postcolonial period was often hard to achieve, as many nations were home to diverse ethnic groups. These people had their own territories and seldom spoke the same language or had the same customs and traditions. Artificial borders put in place by colonial powers—without regard for traditional homelands—also played a huge role. These and other issues created a political tinderbox, especially in nations where one ethnic group economically, politically, and socially dominated the others.

To complicate matters, many of these nations were caught in a geopolitical tug of war between Western democracies and the Soviet Union as each superpower sought to export its ideology to the continent, especially during the decolonization process, when the future allegiance of newly independent nations still seemed up for grabs. The Soviet Union, for example, gave military and economic support to the governments of Angola and Mozambique, while the West supported Kenya, Somalia, and Zaire, among others. These countries' proxy wars, in which the two sides wielded power on behalf of their interests, contributed to massive devastation and human suffering.

The West often acted in its own self-interest, ignoring long-established racism and minority rule among its African allies, especially in South Africa. In that country, apartheid, a system of legally enforced racial **segregation**, kept the white minority and anticommunist **regime** in control. Moreover, in Western-supported Rhodesia, the white minority refused to share power with the black majority. When Portugal gave up its colonies in Angola and Mozambique in 1975 after a long, bitter struggle, the Cold War rivalry between the Soviets and the West fueled a bitter civil war, with each side supporting different factions.

As the Cold War wound down, Africa was still a bubbling cauldron of ethnic resentments, especially in Rwanda and Burundi, where tensions between the Tutsis and Hutus escalated into genocide. Both spoke the same language, but they had different traditions. Further, Belgium alternately favored one side over the other under colonial rule, until 1962, when the Hutus were in power in Rwanda at the time of independence; many Tutsis fled to neighboring Burundi at this point, escaping discrimination or worse under the Hutu regime. In April 1994, the government in Rwanda was still controlled by Hutus, many of whom were extreme in their anti-Tutsi views. Sparked by the downing of a plane in Rwanda carrying Burundi's Hutu president, the Hutu leadership in Rwanda began a massacre of Tutsis and moderate Hutus. By July, however, Tutsi forces had taken control of Rwanda. And, while the genocide was largely over, Tutsi forces were involved in reprisal killings of Hutus, many of whom fled across the border to neighboring countries, especially Zaire. Those who were accused of war crimes during the genocide, including the use of rape as a weapon of war, faced an international court to answer for their actions. In 2005 both groups agreed to a new government that allowed each to participate.

The courtyard of the Genocide Memorial Church in Karongi-Kibuye, in western Rwanda, in 2012.

Genocide also took place in Sudan, where Arab Muslims in the north dominated the non-Muslim population in the south. Beginning in 1955, rebel groups in the south fought against the Muslim government. The fighting even spilled over into neighboring Chad. The conflict killed millions. In 2011, South Sudan declared its independence.

Conflict in Other Areas

During the early years of the twenty-first century, ethnic conflicts continued to spread. In many nations, such as those in South and Central America, indigenous communities strived for more political power and greater economic inclusion.

In 2006 Evo Morales became the first indigenous president in Bolivian history. He soon embarked on a series of health, education, and housing reforms. The country passed a new constitution in 2009 aimed at empowering Bolivia's indigenous communities, which had been marginalized for centuries.

Yet, tension continued, with aboriginal leaders accusing the government of political persecution as Bolivia sought to extract oil on indigenous lands. The government said it needed the oil to finance social programs. Critics argued the policies were not only unsustainable and caused immediate harm to the environment but were damaging to indigenous culture as well.

Elsewhere, ethnic tensions fueled xenophobia in many European nations, especially Germany, France, and Great Britain, who found themselves in the middle of mass migrations from Asia, the Middle East, Eastern Europe, and Africa. As discussed later, the migrants came looking for new jobs, new homes, and more security.

Evo Morales, the president of Bolivia, at the UN climate change conference in Paris, on November 30, 2015.

Text-Dependent Questions

1. What is an ethnonationalist?
2. In what year did Slovenia declare its independence?
3. When did Nelson Mandela become president of South Africa?

Research Projects

1. Use the Internet or library to research images of the struggle against apartheid in South Africa and create a computer slide show depicting that struggle in chronological order.
2. Use this site to study migration routes from each country in the world to the United States: http://migrationsmap.net/#/USA/arrivals. Pick five countries from the drop-down menu to see the routes of migration from those countries. Compare the "arrivals" and "departures." What can you conclude?

Educational Video

Morales Likely to Win Bolivia's Presidential Election
Page 30

Page 30

A news report on the reasons behind the popularity of Evo Morales, Bolivia's first indigenous president.

Published on YouTube by CCTV America. https://youtu.be/36Gk2os9OG8.

WORDS TO UNDERSTAND

collectivism: political system marked by collective control over production and distribution and prioritizing the good of society over the individual.

defrocked: describing the removal of a priest's religious status and authority.

heretics: people whose opinions violate established religious teachings.

secularism: viewpoint that religion and politics should be separate.

Zionism: movement originally for the establishment of a Jewish homeland in Palestine, and later for the support of modern Israel.

ABOVE: The Dome of the Rock, in Jerusalem's Old City, one of the holiest sites for both Muslims and Jews. The Western Wall—an ancient part of Jerusalem's early construction—is in the foreground.

CHAPTER 4

Religious Minorities in the Postwar World

The centuries-old struggle for religious freedom has been ongoing and ever changing. During the Cold War, religion began to play a larger role in world affairs as it became a recognized individual right after the unspeakable death and carnage created by the Holocaust. Religion was also a central theme in the postwar power struggle between the superpowers and often served as a demarcation line between good and evil.

Religion and the Cold War

At the time, many pro-democracy westerners considered the atheistic communists inherently wicked. American presidents, including Franklin Roosevelt, Harry Truman, and Dwight D. Eisenhower, perpetuated this narrative, often framing U.S. foreign policy in religious terms. "Where freedom of religion has been attacked, the attack has come from sources opposed to democracy," Roosevelt said. Truman rallied leaders of many faiths to fight communism, while Eisenhower saw religion, specifically Christianity, as a tool to help peoples resist communism, especially in the Third World.

From their point of view, communists believed that religion had no role under communism. Communist regimes, including those in the Soviet Union, China, and Cambodia, murdered millions during the Cold War because of their religious beliefs. In China, the Communist Party converted temples, mosques, and churches into public buildings. In Cambodia, Pol Pot, leader of the Khmer Rouge, **defrocked** Buddhist monks and forced Muslims to eat pork, which Islam prohibited. At the same time, however, the Soviet-controlled regime in Poland accommodated religion, since it would have been impossible to control the country if it had tried to abolish Catholicism. Indeed, communist opposition to religion depended upon local conditions and the reality on the ground. By the 1990s, in fact, Catholicism had hastened the demise of European communism. The elevation of a Polish priest named Karol Wojtyla to pope of the Catholic Church (as John Paul II) inspired many to work toward the elimination of communist rule.

The Tuol Sleng Genocide Museum, in Phnom Penh, which chronicles the genocide in Cambodia under the Communist leader Pol Pot.

In other parts of the world, religion underwent a revival of sorts. In Latin America, the Catholic Church became a potent political voice. In Western Europe, Christian Democrats, who mixed conservative politics with religious theology, served as a bulwark against communism. Also, however, **secularism** rose in Western Europe after the 1950s and helped to shape not just politics but many aspects of culture and society in countries such as France, Belgium, and Germany. In the Soviet Union, Jews constantly battled for human rights, while in many places in Africa, political, religious, and economic tensions among Muslims, atheistic Marxists, and Christians threw the continent into conflict. In Asia, Buddhism pushed along independence movements in many countries regardless of whether those countries were pro-Soviet or pro-American.

The Troubles of Northern Ireland

One of the most contentious religious struggles in recent European history has been the conflict in Northern Ireland between Catholics and Protestants. The roots of the conflict are not only mired in religion but also in economics and politics. Although most of Ireland had won its freedom from Great Britain in 1922, the northern part of the island, where Protestants outnumbered Catholics, remained under British control.

While Catholics wished to be reunited with the rest of Ireland (dominated by Catholics), the Protestants wanted to remain part of the United Kingdom. Moreover,

Signs of conflict in Belfast, Northern Ireland, around 1970.

the Catholic minority demanded equal rights. They were economically and politically oppressed by the Protestant ruling class. Protestants had the best jobs, brighter futures, and better wages.

As a result, Catholic paramilitary organizations, such as the Irish Republican Army, sought to throw the British out and reunite Northern Ireland with the rest of the country. Periodic outbursts of violence occurred in the decades after independence, but a full-scale civil conflict, known as "the Troubles," did not begin until the late 1960s and
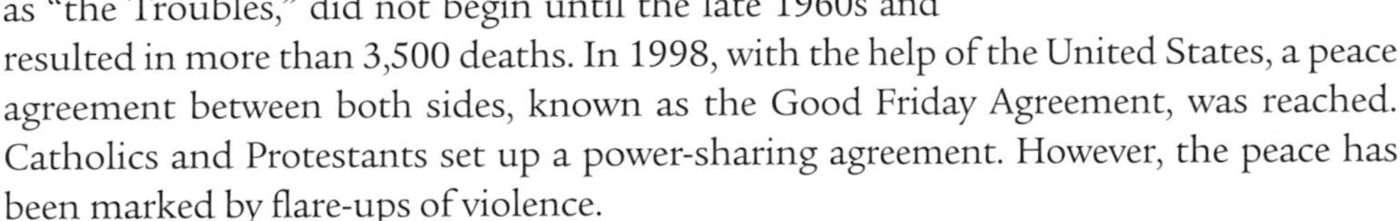
resulted in more than 3,500 deaths. In 1998, with the help of the United States, a peace agreement between both sides, known as the Good Friday Agreement, was reached. Catholics and Protestants set up a power-sharing agreement. However, the peace has been marked by flare-ups of violence.

THE ATHEIST AND THE POPE

In 1988, Soviet president Mikhail Gorbachev saw the impact religion was playing in Eastern Europe, including the Soviet Union. Although he was an avowed atheist, Gorbachev signaled an openness to Soviets still attached to the region's Christian traditions.

Gorbachev even visited Pope John Paul II in the Vatican, marking an end to the traditional tension between Moscow and Rome. When introducing his wife, Raisa, to the pope, the Soviet leader said, "Raisa Maximovna, I have the honor to introduce the highest moral authority on Earth."

Islam in the Postwar World

The European colonization of Muslim territories in the Middle East and Africa began in the nineteenth century and continued well past World War I (1914–1918), when Europe's colonial powers carved up the Ottoman Empire. At the end of the Second World War, with European colonialism disappearing, Islam was the dominant religion in already independent states. And in fact, many Muslim countries—Arab and non-Arab—pursued modernization models provided by the West or the communist world: nationalism, capitalism, and **collectivism**. Religion was not paramount.

In colonized Muslim territories in the Middle East, sub-Saharan Africa, and Southeast Asia, the legacy of colonialism remained after independence was gained, as was the case in other newly independent countries. The influence of colonialism would shape the politics of these new states and toss these regions into a seemingly endless series of conflicts, many perpetuated by the superpowers. For example, oil made the Middle East a prime battleground.

The West eyed the Middle East not only for the oil, but also as a strategic region that could help contain Soviet expansion. The United States and its allies sought to impress upon the Muslim world that the Soviets were their common enemies. But things were unpredictable in the region, especially after Egypt's nationalist president, Gamal Abdel Nasser, tried to follow a path independent from the West and established a relationship with the Soviets. Consequently, the United States began looking for groups it could work with. One was the Muslim Brotherhood in Egypt, a one-time supporter of Nasser.

The group, made up of Islamist intellectuals, had a falling out with Nasser after it became clear he did not want to create an Islamic state, as the Brotherhood had hoped. Nasser cracked down on the Brotherhood, viewing them as a threat to his nationalist, procommunist regime. The United States reached out to the Brotherhood, which became an ally in the region, at least during the period before Islamic extremism and terrorism began to shape U.S. foreign policy.

The United States also looked to Saudi Arabia. The Saudi royal family was devoutly hostile to the Soviets. In fact, the Saudis did not even have diplomatic relations with Moscow. The Saudi ruling family, however, compromised with the Wahhabi religious establishment. Wahhabism, an ultraconservative form of Islam, was fueled by petrodollars—money earned in the international oil trade. In the 1970s, it helped lead the spread of the ultraconservative strand of Sunni Islam across the Muslim world.

The situation was even more complicated due to creation of the modern Jewish state of Israel in 1948 in Palestine. At that time, Muslim Arabs, who lived in what was once British-controlled Palestine, looked upon the UN action as illegal. They rejected the idea of a Jewish state on territory the Arabs believed was rightfully theirs. The two sides would spend the next several decades fighting over territory, creating one of the most unstable regions in the world. Eventually, the conflict increased rivalries in the

A small village on a hill sits behind the wall separating the West Bank, a Palestinian area, and Israel.

region, splintering the Arab world. Egypt and Jordan, for example, recognized Israel's right to exist in 1970, while other countries, including Libya and Iraq, did not.

The Cold War superpowers also contributed to the complexities surrounding the Palestinian-Israeli conflict. Israel was supported by the United States, Great Britain, and other Western countries. And the West's support for Israel often led to Soviet support for Israel's Arab enemies. For instance, in 1953 the Soviet Union cut relations with Israel and supported Egypt.

Yet local forces usually proved more powerful than superpower schemes. The rulers of Egypt, first Nasser and then Anwar Sadat, are good examples, as are the difficulties the Soviets experienced during its involvement in and subsequent invasion of Afghanistan in the 1970s and 1980s, when it fought for influence there against the Islamic mujahideen. In another layer of complexity, Jews inside the Soviet Union who supported Israel were labeled traitors and often persecuted. Jewish organizations in Russia were shut down, as were most synagogues. Soviet propaganda against the Jews was racist, as the government called **Zionism** a "world threat."

At the same time, a series of nationalistic movements emerged throughout the Islamic world. Radical Muslims began to use terrorism as a means to achieve political goals. Groups that supported Palestinians against Israel, such as al-Fatah and the Popular Front for the Liberation of Palestine, were able to spread their brand of terrorism, which was directed primarily against Israel but also against its Western supporters abroad.

Moreover, many Islamic groups and secular nationalists battled one another to fill the void left by the lack of government resources that emerged after the colonial powers had left and outside modernization models appeared to have failed. Religious groups provided people with food, health care, and education–things many conservative Arab regimes could not provide. Sometimes, such as in Saudi Arabia, the government turned to Islamic groups, such as the Muslim Brotherhood, to act as a counterweight to nationalist movements.

Shiite versus Sunni

The Middle East also teemed with religious hostilities that went back centuries. One of the most divisive was the Muslim split between Shiite (Shia) and Sunni over who would be Muhammad's successor. This split occurred soon after the death of the Prophet Muhammad in 632 and took place in present-day Saudi Arabia. The Shiites believed that the Prophet's heir should come from Muhammad's family. The Sunnis believed the new Muslim leader should be the person who was the best leader.

Tensions between both sides often erupted in conflict. The split would turn out to be one of the most powerful drivers of violence in the Middle East since the end of World War II. In many Muslim countries, the Shiites were the minority, although they were the majority in Iran, Iraq, Bahrain, and some parts of the Soviet Union, such as

Azerbaijan. The Shiites often lived in the poorest sections in countries governed by Sunnis and viewed themselves as being oppressed and discriminated against. Sunni extremists consider the Shia **heretics**.

Sectarian violence between the two groups exploded in 1979 and acquired a new, geopolitical dimension when Iranian Shiite extremists seized control from the shah, the country's secular U.S.–leaning monarch, during the Iranian Revolution. The revolution in Iran was perceived as a threat to conservative Sunni regimes in the area, including the one in nearby Iraq. As a result, Iraq invaded Iran in 1980, starting a protracted war between the two countries that lasted until 1988 and resulted in half a million casualties.

Since then, the Sunni-Shiite division has stoked other tensions in the region. Today, Iran supports Shiite regimes and militias beyond its borders in Lebanon, Syria, Iraq, and in other countries. And Saudi Arabia supports Sunni regimes in Sudan and Bahrain, as well as militant groups throughout the region. Further, each group has tens of thousands of organized sectarian militants in the Middle East, and many have spawned terrorists groups and networks, such as the Sunni-oriented al-Qaeda and ISIS, or the Islamic State, which some say the Saudi royal family has funded. Experts fear the split between Sunni and Shiite could trigger a broader conflict. In 2016 the Sunni royal family in Saudi Arabia announced the execution of forty-seven people for terrorism, including a Shiite cleric. The Shiite community, led by Iran, denounced the execution, increasing anxiety in an already tension-filled region.

A scene from the Iranian Revolution in Shahyad Square in the capital, Tehran.

Text-Dependent Questions

1. When did Israel become a state?
2. What are the two main sects of Islam?
3. When did Ireland achieve its independence?

Research Projects

1. Write the history of one of the religious conflicts mentioned in this chapter. Make a timeline of the major events defining the conflict and steps taken, if any, to settle it.
2. Research the population of all of the world's major religions. Then create either a pie chart or a bar graph comparing each population. You can also create a chart or graph that focuses on just one region, such as the Middle East, North America, China, Southeast Asia, or Europe.

WORDS TO UNDERSTAND

assimilation: adoption of the traits and characteristics of a larger group or person by a newly arrived group or person.

demographers: people who study human populations.

inclusion: becoming part of a group.

pluralism: existence of different groups and ideas in a society.

stereotyping: oversimplifying the traits of a person or group, sometimes involving inaccuracies.

ABOVE: Oxford Street in London in 2015. The crowds of people show the city to be one of the most multicultural of any in the world.

CHAPTER

5

Multiculturalism and Globalization

Multiculturalism, the coexistence and acceptance of multiple cultural traditions, is not a new concept. Various linguistic, ethnic, and religious groups have mingled and lived with one another for centuries. But in the aftermath of World War II, a new age of multiculturalism emerged as the modern era of globalization began to take shape.

The very global nature of the war, bringing different peoples into contact and conflict, set the stage for the growing awareness of individual groups and their rights. And the decolonization that followed the war unleashed ethnic rivalries once tamped down by colonial power structures (as discussed in the previous chapters). These conflicts raised awareness of how multifaceted many modern nations of the world are—ethnically, racially, and religiously. The intensity, violence, and in some cases destructiveness of these conflicts, indeed, continued to bring minority and religious rights to the foreground of international relations and domestic politics. At the same time, as globalizing forces—migration, communication, and trade among nations—increased, awareness of how culturally, religiously, and ethnically complex the world's people were increased as well.

The Multicultural Debate

In the postwar world, the idea of fostering multicultural **inclusion** has been supported by the United Nations. In the aftermath of World War II, it was keenly motivated by a desire to promote international cooperation to protect the rights of the individual after the horrors of the Holocaust. With such motivations in mind, Article 22 of the UN's Universal Declaration of Human Rights stated, "Everyone, as a member of society, has the right to social security and is entitled to realization, through national effort and international co-operation and in accordance with the organization and resources of each State, of the economic, social and cultural rights indispensable for his dignity and the free development of his personality."

WHAT IS MULTICULTURALISM?

Multiculturalism has many faces. It can mirror the actual **pluralism** in a society, reflecting different languages, cultures, and ethnicities. It can also be a political philosophy through which all people, regardless of ethnic or religious backgrounds, are considered equal. Multiculturalism can also be used by governments to encourage pluralism through public policy, such as requiring teachers to highlight the struggles of minorities in history. Despite multiculturalism's many benefits, there has been a vociferous debate over its merits in an increasingly globalized world.

Philippines ambassador signing the International Covenant on Civil and Political Rights in 1966.

Further, the UN put in place a variety of programs to cultivate and protect minority groups. The UN's commitment to multiculturalism was subsequently echoed in Article 27 of the 1966 International Covenant on Civil and Political Rights, which stated that "In those States in which ethnic, religious, or linguistic minorities exist, persons belonging to such minorities should not be denied the right, in community with the other members of their group, to enjoy their own culture, to profess and practice their own religion, or to use their own language." Sixteen years later, the UN's Declaration on the Rights of Persons Belonging to National or Ethnic, Religious and Linguistic Minorities reaffirmed those rights.

Yet critics say attempts by the UN and others to promote diversity have, in effect, produced more racism and **stereotyping**. In their view, multiculturalism isolates ethnic groups, allowing them to focus on their own agendas instead of society writ large. That, critics say, leads to disunity and conflict. They point to educational reforms in the United States that mandate that schools teach alternative perspectives of history, which opponents say undermines the foundations of Western civilization.

Some mainstream politicians, including British prime minister David Cameron and German chancellor Angela Merkel, have publicly denounced multiculturalism because it has fueled the rise of far-right, populist politicians along with acts of violence. Even in the United States, multiculturalism has become a catchall for immigration policy, the angst of the white middle class, and other political and social issues.

At times, the rhetoric has become heated. Donald Trump, one of the major U.S. presidential candidates in 2016, even called for a "temporary" ban on Muslims coming into the United States because of fears of terrorism. He also called for building a wall across the entire southern U.S. border to keep Mexicans and others from illegally entering the United States, an idea that is popular among some in the U.S. electorate.

Catholicism's leader Pope Francis (center) meeting with Prince Ghazi (left), advisor to the king of Jordan on religious and cultural affairs, at Jerusalem's Temple Mount, one of the holiest sites in the world for Christians, Jews, and Muslims.

In the view of others, however, multiculturalism is not the bogeyman that many fear. The problem, they say, is not that there's too much diversity, but too much racism. In their view, multiculturalism promotes acceptance as people become familiar with new cultures and traditions. For the newcomers, interacting with others in their new communities diminishes the importance of their birth country, as their actions are based on how to thrive in their adopted homeland.

Additionally, multiculturalism allows different groups to form relationships, share traditions, and enrich communities. These groups do not become isolated, nor do they turn inward. Instead, they seek to contribute to their new nation's economic, social, and cultural makeup.

Coming to Terms with Multiculturalism

As globalization became more entrenched in the aftermath of World War II, nations had to find ways to deal with the influx of newcomers from different backgrounds who moved from their homelands in search of new economic opportunities or to escape persecution. In many instances, they competed with local citizens for food, housing, water, land, health care, and limited resources. These and other reasons conspired to fuel hatred among many natives, making **assimilation** for many groups difficult. Each nation had to find new mechanisms to deal with these and other issues. Some countries were successful, others were not.

After World War II, large numbers of immigrants from many former British colonies, including India and Pakistan, moved to Great Britain in search of a better life. While the government welcomed the migrants as a source of new labor, some Britons were concerned that the immigrants would challenge traditional "Britishness," a largely racial concept that gave the British, especially the country's elite, a sense of self-worth and identity. The Colonial Office in 1955 even issued a report warning that "a large coloured community as a noticeable feature of our social life would weaken . . . the concept of England or Britain to which people of British stock throughout the Commonwealth are attached."

During the 1960s, the British passed laws to exclude some ethnic minorities. By the 1970s and 1980s, race riots engulfed several British cities as racial tensions overheated. At that time, ethnic minorities began to oppose Britain's discriminatory immigration controls. Each struggled for political and economic equality. A government report said that while the riots were spontaneous, they were nevertheless created by "complex political, social, and economic factors."

The riots served as a wake-up call. In response, many British leaders developed a new set of strategies to help foster equal opportunity in ethnic communities. These programs allowed different peoples to express their own culture, history, and values. For the most part, the transition worked. Ethnic communities were encouraged not only to embrace Britain as their home, but also to look inward as confirmation of who they were as a people. Britain slowly became an increasingly multicultural society. From 1993 to 2013, the number of foreign-born people in the United Kingdom

A demonstrator in London on March 21, 2015, during an antiracism march in honor of the annual UN International Day for the Elimination of Racial Discrimination.

increased from 3.8 million to 7.9 million, according to the University of Oxford. Most had come from India, Poland, Pakistan, and Ireland. Despite these trends, Britain still struggles with assimilating its immigrant population. The 2005 suicide bombings in the London subway by Islamic terrorists exemplify the challenges Britain faces. By 2015 the number of foreign-born had passed 8 million, as an influx of Syrian war refugees moved to Britain to be resettled. As with many countries dealing with the 2015–2016 migration crisis, whether Britain can fully accept and assimilate them is an open question.

Multiculturalism in Germany

Globalization also changed Germany, a once homogenous society that had radically shifted to a more pluralistic nation after the Cold War. As Germany became an economic powerhouse during the 1960s and 1970s, newcomers, especially from the Mediterranean region, began flocking to its borders in the hopes of making a decent living. Many came from Turkey, Italy, Morocco, and Portugal. They came as "guest workers," arriving at a time when there was a great labor shortage in the country. Turkey contributed the most workers. The Turks ultimately formed the largest ethnic minority in the country, with nearly 2.7 million people, according to a 2009 study by the German Interior Ministry, published in Germany's *Citizen News*.

Although Germany needed these guest workers, the country did not accept them as full members of society. The government never intended the immigrants to stay and did not provide them with a path to citizenship, leading to deep-seated mistrust on both sides. The influx of the foreigners had become a source of concern for native Germans, who feared the immigrants were taking away their jobs and driving wages down. The natives also resented the newcomers, believing they were not doing enough to learn the language and assimilate. Gradually, after unification in 1990, the government began to address some of these issues; for example, it relaxed rules on dual-citizenship for people born in Germany to migrant parents.

By 2015, Germany had opened its doors once again, this time to those fleeing the war-torn Middle East and

According to Harvard researchers, Africa is home to the most diverse population on the planet, while Australia, Scandinavia, France, and Italy, among others, are the least diverse. The researchers classified each country's diversity by asking people how they view themselves ethnically.

Within Africa, the nations of the sub-Sahara are the most diverse. Uganda tops the list, and Liberia comes in second. Researchers said part of the reason is the way Europeans carved the continent during the colonial period. They formed borders with little regard for the cultures of the people who lived there. When these countries achieved independence, the borders remained, as did the different ethnic, religious, and linguistic groups inside each nation.

Afghanistan. The influx of refugees, especially from Syria, resulted in a backlash in some places. Right-wing groups resented the refugees, and a wave of xenophobia spread across the country. That said, many Germans—under the moral leadership of Prime Minister Angela Merkel, who has worked hard to get the members of the European Union to address the crisis—have gone to great lengths to welcome and help the refugees.

Problems in Quebec

In 1971, Canada became the first country to adopt multiculturalism as an official government policy. In the process, the government institutionalized the equality of all Canadian citizens regardless of their racial, religious, linguistic, or ethnic origins. The policy ensured that all Canadians were equal before the law and in opportunity. These policy pronouncements came as the country's immigrant communities were expanding and becoming more diverse. In the second half of the twentieth century, as a result of legislation easing immigration restrictions in the 1960s, Canada welcomed more people from non-European countries than it ever had, including migrants from Asia, Africa, and the Caribbean. Multiculturalism as a national policy reflected Canada's new reality.

While the country might have seemed like a multicultural utopia, however, separatists in Quebec sought political sovereignty, claiming that the French-speaking province was culturally distinct from the rest of Canada. The movement for Quebec's independence from Canada, which has waxed and waned over the decades, has been seen as the best way to preserve the province's language, religion, and cultural identity.

A sign in Canada opposing ("NON") a 1995 referendum on Quebec's independence from Canada.

Unlike the rest of Canada, Quebec has taken a dim view of multiculturalism. In 1997 the province made French its official and only language. And the province refused to ratify a clause in the country's 1982 constitution stating the need to preserve "the multicultural heritage of Canadians." In 2013, Quebec lawmakers also introduced a bill, the Quebec Charter of Values, banning any display of "ostentatious" religious symbols, such as veils and "large" crosses, by public employees.

The law, which did not pass, would have put many public employees, who were also members of religious minority groups, in the position of having to decide whether to acquiesce or move to a different province. The measure's introduction came on the heels of the Canadian government's creation of the Office of Religious Freedom, which was charged to "protect, and advocate on behalf of religious minorities under threat," and to "promote Canadian values of pluralism and tolerance abroad."

The American Experience

Multiculturalism is ingrained in the American psyche, as the United States has absorbed (sometimes reluctantly) streams of immigrants from all corners of the world. Poles, Irish, Italians, Chinese, Mexicans, Germans, Vietnamese, and others moved to the United States for a variety of reasons. Some were escaping political and religious persecution. Others hoped to share in America's economic success. These first-generation immigrants often held on to their old identity, while second generations became strictly "Americans."

While the United States has been thought of as a land of open arms, the country has always regulated the flow of immigrants into the country. In the twentieth century, from the 1920s to the passage of the 1965 Immigration and Naturalization Act, country-of-origin quotas had been the main determinant of who was allowed in. The Emergency Quota Act, passed in 1921, also set an overall limit on the number of immigrants. With the 1965 act, those with skills needed in the U.S. economy, plus those with existing relationships with U.S. citizens and residents, were given priority. The country since then has struggled to enact comprehensive immigration reform, an effort by many to recognize legally the huge number of immigrants that have come in, largely across the southern border with Mexico.

Xenophobia has been a constant feature of the U.S. response to immigration, despite the fact that it is such a prominent social and demographic factor throughout U.S. history. Overt racism and institutional discrimination have been commonplace, marginalizing many communities. By the 1970s, many immigrant groups began to assert their identity, as they began to see themselves as separate political and social units, giving rise to "identity politics." Spurred on by the successes of the civil rights movement, these groups began to gain their own power. Consequently, Native Americans, African Americans, women, and lesbians and gays, among others, began

Chinatown in New York City. Like many major world cities, New York has a vibrant community of Chinese, Thai, and other Asian immigrants.

demanding more social, economic, and political acceptance. An increasing emphasis on identity politics has continued to shape U.S. political life well beyond the 1970s.

Twenty-first century demographics, which show an increasingly multiethnic United States, may well enhance this trend. According to the U.S. Census Bureau, as of 2015, 62.1 percent of the nation was white, while 13 percent considered themselves black or African American. Hispanics made up 17.4 percent of the population, and Asian Americans made up 5.6 percent. Thirty-five years earlier, 80 percent of Americans were white, 6 percent were Hispanic, and 12 percent were black.

Demographers believe the trend will continue and that by 2060, whites will be less than 44 percent of the population, while the Hispanic population will be 29 percent. Nothing illustrates this better than the rise of "majority-minority states," in which minority groups have become the majority of that state's population. As of 2015, minorities were the majority in four states, including: California, Hawaii, New Mexico, and Texas. As the years pass, experts say, more states will follow.

Text-Dependent Questions

1. Describe the general idea behind Article 22 of the Universal Declaration of Human Rights.
2. Which immigrant group in Germany is the largest?
3. Which country was the first to adopt multiculturalism as an official government policy?

Research Projects

1. Research how different ethnic groups have affected your community. Present your findings to your class in the form of an oral presentation.
2. Create a survey asking your classmates what their ethnic backgrounds are. Tabulate what you find and present your findings to your class.

Educational Video

London 7/7 Attacks: How the Day Unfolded
Page 45

A montage of news footage compiled by the BBC on the coordinated suicide bombings on July 7, 2005, in London; meant for broadcast ten years after the attacks.

Published on YouTube by BBC News. https://youtu.be/gwyqT7rcCYk.

WORDS TO UNDERSTAND

crimes against humanity: widespread atrocities committed against an identified group of people and carried out under the approval of a government.

gender inequality: unequal treatment based on a person's gender.

institutional: relating to the systematic policy of an agency or country.

mantra: a motto or slogan that encapsulates a value or idea important to a person or group.

ABOVE: Malala Yousafzai (left), a young woman attacked by the Pakistani Taliban, for insisting on getting an education, has become a worldwide symbol of women and girl's rights. Here, she is being interviewed during the 2014 Women of the World Festival.

CHAPTER

6

The Current Scene

Minority rights, ethnic rights, indigenous rights, women's rights—these individual strands have come together in the postwar world, as seen in these chapters, in a way that presents both progress and challenges. The struggle of these groups for recognition and power is reflected in the way group activism takes place on a global stage. And even though minority activists sometimes criticize the effects of globalization, they have used the international stage to effect change in powerful ways.

No part of this story reflects today's changing social fabric as well as that of women. Indeed, the changing political, economic, and social status of women goes hand in hand with how the empowerment of ethnic and religious minorities has changed social structures in the twenty-first century.

Women's Changing Roles

In December 2015, *Time* magazine named German chancellor Angela Merkel its "Person of the Year." Merkel, who had grown up in communist East Germany during the Cold War, had, in the magazine's words, become the "de facto leader of the European Union, the most prosperous joint venture on the planet." Merkel, the magazine said, navigated Germany and the rest of the EU through several financial and political crises. She also threw Germany's doors open to tens of thousands of refugees and migrants after other European nations slammed doors in their faces. *Time* wrote:

> By viewing the refugees as victims to be rescued rather than invaders to be repelled, the woman raised behind the Iron Curtain gambled on freedom. The pastor's daughter wielded mercy like a weapon. You can agree with her or not, but she is not taking the easy road. Leaders are tested only when people don't want to follow.

While the achievements of individual women such as Merkel have marked advances in the long history of women's rights, women as a group have not achieved

Liberian president Ellen Johnson Sirleaf with then–U.S. secretary of state, Hillary Clinton, at a meeting in Washington, D.C., in 2011.

parity with men in parliaments and other world legislatures. To be sure, impressive advances have been made. And, as a surprise to many, some of these are in the developing world. In 2015, two African women led their national governments: the Central African Republic's president, Catherine Samba-Panza, appointed in 2014; and Liberia's president, Ellen Johnson Sirleaf, elected in 2006. The tiny African country of Rwanda, as seen in the accompanying table, leads the world in women's representation in legislatures.

Despite these advances, in many of today's societies, women are still looked upon as second-class citizens. They are often victims of violence and unjust traditions. They are excluded from participating fully in economic life. After decades of fighting for equal rights and equal pay, women are a long way from being on the same economic footing with men. According to UN Women, the United Nations entity for gender equality and the empowerment of women, **gender inequality** is a major cause of hunger and poverty. Less than 20 percent of the world's landowners are women. Women in sub-Saharan Africa spend about 40 billion hours a year collecting water.

In many countries, women are not only on the lowest rung of the economic ladder, they also do not have the same educational opportunities as men. Women account for two-thirds of the world's 796 million illiterate people. Compared to girls from urban areas, girls from rural areas are twice as likely not to go to school.

Share of Seats Held by Women in National Parliaments
Top Ten, as of December 1, 2015

Rank	Country	Lower or Single House			Upper House or Senate		
		Total Seats	Women Holding Seats	Percent	Total Seats	Women Holding Seats	Percent of Seats
1	Rwanda	80	51	63.8%	26	10	38.5%
2	Bolivia	130	69	53.1%	36	17	47.2%
3	Cuba	612	299	48.9%	---	---	---
4	Seychelles	32	14	43.8%	---	---	---
5	Sweden	349	152	43.6%	---	---	---
6	Senegal	150	64	42.7%	---	---	---
7	Mexico	498	211	42.4%	128	43	33.6%
8	South Africa	400	168	42.0%	54	19	35.2%
9	Ecuador	137	57	41.6%	---	---	---
10	Finland	200	83	41.5%	---	---	---

Source: "Women in National Parliaments," Inter-Parliamentary Union (http://www.ipu.org/wmn-e/classif.htm#1).

Millennium Goals

As the turn of the century approached, the United Nations Development Programme developed a series of Millennium Development Goals (MDGs) to combat poverty, hunger, disease, illiteracy, environmental damage, and discrimination against women. These goals, put into place at the start of the new millennium in 2000, were designed not only to address human development issues, but also to provide a framework for the UN's economic development efforts. The eight MDGs were designed to be both measurable and achievable.

Although six of the eight goals mention women and girls as priority targets, progress has been slow. According to the MDG 2015 report, women face discrimination at work and are more likely than men to live in poverty. While poverty rates have declined around the world, the ratio of women to men in poor households in Latin America and the Caribbean increased from 108 women for every 100 men in 1997 to 117 women for every 100 men in 2012. In addition, women earn 24 percent less than men.

UN Women predicts it will take nearly another half century before women achieve political parity with men, and nearly eighty years before women are equal to men in terms of economic progress.

IN THEIR OWN WORDS

Githu Muigai, Attorney General of the Republic of Kenya

Racism and xenophobia are not yesterday's problems; they remain an immense challenge for today. Be it the member of an ethnic minority who is attacked or killed in the context of a conflict due to his or her minority status; the individual subjected to stop and searches, interrogations, or arrests solely because of his or her perceived religious or ethnic background; the migrant, the refugee, or asylum-seeker who faces daily discrimination due to his or her status as a non-citizen; or the football player who is insulted because of his skin color—all these people unfortunately demonstrate the validity of my statement.

—Presenting two reports on racism to the United Nations in 2010.

Yet there have been some successes. The 2015 MDG reports the following statistics:

- More girls are now in school compared to fifteen years ago.
- Women now make up 41 percent of paid workers, an increase of 35 percent since 1990.
- Women are represented in nearly 90 percent of 174 parliamentary governments.
- The mortality rate for mothers has declined by 45 percent since 1990.
- In North Africa, 89 percent of pregnant women now receive better health care than they did in 1990, while 11 percent more women aged fifteen to forty-nine now use contraception to avoid pregnancy.

Status of Ethnic and Religious Minorities

According to the Minority Rights Group International's Peoples under Threat index, many countries, including Syria, Yemen, and Ukraine, saw a sharp spike in ethnoreligious violence in 2014–2015. One of the worst conflicts was in Myanmar (also referred to as Burma). Although the country's authoritarian government has shown signs of loosening its grip, hostility continues to grow against the country's minority Muslim population, the Rohingya.

In 2013, ethnic tensions between the Rohingya and Rakhine Buddhists, who make up the majority of the country's population, escalated into violence. A study by Yale University suggested that the **institutional** abuse of the Rohingya has amounted to genocide. The Rohingya have been denied citizenship, and hundreds of thousands have been forced from their homes. Others have been forced into labor. Mosques have been burned and women and girls have been raped and held as sex slaves.

While many Latin American countries, such as Bolivia and Ecuador, have made great strides in recognizing indigenous rights in recent years, violence and discrimination has continued. In Peru in 2009, for instance, violence occurred between indigenous protesters and police over the government's refusal to repeal laws that made it easy to turn over indigenous lands to oil and mining companies.

In Brisbane, Australia, members of the Burmese Rohingya Association march in support of the Rohingya in Myanmar, at the World Refugee Rally in June 2015.

Protection of Minority Rights

When the United Nations approved the Universal Declaration of Human Rights in 1948, it gave voice to thousands of minority groups that had been denied basic rights as human beings and repeatedly discriminated against because of race, gender, ethnic, class, religious, cultural, and linguistic differences. The spread of democracy and the rise of globalization forced people and governments to take action to stop human rights abuses. Many organizations and nations took the lead and began to press violators to end abuses. In particular, human rights watchdog groups, such as Amnesty International, Human Rights Watch, and others, began to conduct research on human rights abuses, becoming advocates for those who were discriminated against. Minority Rights Group International began keeping a list of groups around the world that are under attack.

As the years passed, the UN agreed to twenty treaties that further defined and elaborated on human rights, including agreements to end torture and genocide and to help refugees, women, and children. Even regional organizations produced laws and documents safeguarding human rights. The nations of Africa, for example, passed the Charter of Human and Peoples' Rights in 1981, while Muslim states ratified the Cairo Declaration on Human Rights in Islam in 1990.

Yet, despite these and other agreements, human rights abuses continued. In the 1980s, governments, working with one another or individually, started to apply economic pressure—sanctions—to change the actions of governments. Trade and economic sanctions were levied against South Africa, for example, which was forced to end apartheid, partly due to this international pressure.

More than seventy years after the end of World War II, the horrors of that conflict still resonate. The "never again" **mantra** of that terrible time has forced the world to come to grips with the abhorrent actions of governments against minority religious, ethnic, and cultural groups. Much has been done to hold governments and individuals accountable for their actions.

A recent development is the adoption by many UN member states of a new international norm, Responsibility to Protect (R2P), under which not only individual states, but also the international community, pledge to protect populations from **crimes against humanity**. Also, in 2016, the International Criminal Tribunal for the former Yugoslavia convicted Bosnian Serb leader Radovan Karadzic to forty years in jail for his role in the atrocities committed in the 1990s. At the same time, there are many places and conflicts where minorities continue to be under siege, with the outside world either unable or unwilling to intervene. International norms only go so far, even in the twenty-first century. The protection of minority rights requires hard work in many other areas, with economic development, education, and conflict resolution being only the most prominent.

A crowd in Amsterdam, the Netherlands, stands against racism on March 22, 2008.

Text-Dependent Questions

1. What percentage of women own land?
2. Who are the Rohingya?
3. What is Responsibility to Protect (R2P)?

Research Projects

1. Spend a week keeping track of the news by reading newspapers or respected Internet news sites. Create a list of all the stories relating to conflicts involving race, ethnicity, and gender. You can just focus on one country, if you choose. What similarities do you see? What differences are there? What can you conclude?
2. Select one of the women currently leading an African country mentioned in the text. Write a brief biography of her, focusing on the personal and professional pathway that led her to become a national leader.

Timeline

1947	Independence of India from the British Empire uproots some 12 million people and establishes India as a Hindu state and Pakistan as a Muslim state.
1948	The Jewish nation of Israel is created in Palestine, displacing Arabs who live in the territory.
1949	China's new leader, Mao Zedong, enacts a series of reforms that reshape the role of women in Chinese society.
1955	Genocide takes place in Sudan, where Arab Muslims in the north dominate the non-Muslim population in the south; in the next year, rebel groups in the south fight against the Muslim government.
1960	The birth control pill is introduced, allowing women a choice about when to have children.
1960s	A full-scale civil conflict, known as "the Troubles," begins in Northern Ireland between Protestants and Catholics, resulting in more than 3,500 deaths.
	Economic immigrants, especially from the Mediterranean region, begin to arrive in Germany; Britain, among other nations, passes laws to exclude some ethnic minorities; Canada welcomes more people from non-European countries than it ever has.
1963	Betty Friedan's book *The Feminine Mystique* is published, helping to launch modern feminism.
1965	The U.S. Immigration and Naturalization Act passes, ending country-of-origin quotas, in effect since the 1920s.
1966	The UN's commitment to multiculturalism is enshrined in Article 27 of the International Covenant on Civil and Political Rights.
	Indira Gandhi becomes the first woman prime minister of India.
1970s	Wahhabism, an ultraconservative form of Sunni Islam practiced in Saudi Arabia, begins to spread across the Muslim world.
1971	Canada becomes the first country to adopt multiculturalism as an official government policy.
1978	Deng Xiaoping succeeds Mao as leader of China; under his rule, women's status improves greatly.
1979	Shiite extremists seize control from the country's secular U.S.-leaning monarch during the Iranian Revolution.
1980	Sunni Iraq invades Shiite Iran, starting a long war between the two countries that lasts until 1988 and results in half a million casualties.
1981	The nations of Africa pass the Charter of Human and Peoples' Rights.

1990	Muslim states ratify the Cairo Declaration on Human Rights in Islam.
	Germany reunifies and begins to address immigrant issues, including dual-citizenship for people born in Germany to migrant parents.
1994	Hutu leaders in Rwanda begin a massacre of Tutsis and moderate Hutus; Tutsi forces soon take control, and some are involved in reprisal killings of Hutus.
	Apartheid ends in South Africa; citizens of every race are able to vote for the first time and elect black anti-apartheid activist, Nelson Mandela.
	Separatists in Chechnya, home to many ethnic and religious groups, including Muslim Chechens, try to break away from Russian rule, beginning a bloody civil war.
1995	After several EU and UN initiatives fail to stop the ethnic fighting in Bosnia-Herzegovina, NATO intervention and U.S.-led diplomacy result in the "Dayton Accords."
1997	The Canadian province of Quebec makes French its only official language.
1998	The Good Friday Agreement in Northern Ireland is reached between Irish Catholics and Protestants.
2000	The Millennium Development Goals (MDGs) are launched and include empowerment of, and anti-discrimination against, women.
2005	The 2005 suicide bombings in the London subway by Islamic terrorists exemplify the challenges Britain faces in assimilating its Muslim minority population.
2006	Evo Morales becomes the first indigenous president in Bolivian history.
2009	In Peru, violence occurs between indigenous protesters and police over the use of indigenous lands by oil and mining companies.
2013	Ethnic tensions in Myanmar between the Muslim Rohingya and Rakhine Buddhists, who make up the majority of the country's population, escalate into violence.
	Quebec lawmakers introduce the Quebec Charter of Values, banning any display of "ostentatious" religious symbols, such as veils and "large" crosses, by public employees.
2014–2015	According to the Minority Rights Group International's Peoples under Threat index, many countries, including Syria, Yemen, and Ukraine, see a sharp spike in ethnoreligious violence.
2015	Germany has opened its doors to those fleeing the war-torn Middle East and Afghanistan.
	The small African country of Rwanda leads the world in women's representation in legislatures.
2016	The International Criminal Tribunal for the former Yugoslavia convicts Bosnian Serb leader Radovan Karadzic for his role in the ethnic atrocities committed in the 1990s.

Further Research

BOOKS

Allen, James Paul, and Eugene J. Turner. *We the People: An Atlas of American Ethnic Diversity.* London: MacMillian Publishing, 1998.

Kristof, Nicholas D., and Sheryl WuDunn. *Half the Sky: Turning Oppression into Opportunity for Women Worldwide.* New York: Vintage, 2010.

Rattansi, Ali. *Multiculturalism: A Very Short Introduction.* Oxford, UK: Oxford University Press, 2011.

Schaefer, Richard T. *Racial and Ethnic Groups.* 13th ed. New York: Pearson, 2014.

ONLINE

Central Intelligence Agency, "Ethnic Groups": https://www.cia.gov/library/publications/the-world-factbook/fields/2075.html.

Human Rights Watch: "Women's Rights": https://www.hrw.org/topic/womens-rights.

Office of the United Nations High Commissioner for Refugees (OHCHR): http://www.ohchr.org/EN/Pages/Home.aspx.

UN Women: http://www.unwomen.org/en.

NOTE TO EDUCATORS: This book contains both imperial and metric measurements as well as references to global practices and trends in an effort to encourage the student to gain a worldly perspective. We, as publishers, feel it's our role to give young adults the tools they need to thrive in a global society.

Index

Italicized page numbers refer to illustrations

Index (continued)

Photo Credits

Page number	Page location	Archive/Photographer
8	Top	iStock/ElenaMirage
10	Top	National Archives and Records Administration/Lt. Arnold E. Samuelson
11	Bottom	National Archives and Records Administration/Franklin D. Roosevelt Library
12	Bottom	Library of Congress Prints and Photographs Division
14	Top	Library of Congress/Thomas J. O'Halloran
15	Bottom	Shutterstock/Everett Collection
16	Bottom	Wikimedia Commons/U.S. Air Force
17	Top	Wikimedia Commons/Malchish.org
18	Top	iStock/HultonArchive
19	Bottom	Shutterstock/Everett Historical
20	Bottom	Wikimedia Commons/Dutch National Archives
21	Top left	Library of Congress/Warren K. Leffler
21	Top right	Library of Congress/Fred Palumbo
22	Bottom	Shutterstock/Saikat Paul
24	Top	Shutterstock/Bill Anastasiou
26	Bottom	Wikimedia Commons/Mikhail Evstafiev
27	Top	Shutterstock/Northfoto
29	Top	Wikimedia Commons/Adam Jones, Ph.D.
30	Bottom	Shutterstock/Frederic Legrand - COMEO
32	Top	Shutterstock/Ryan Rodrick Beiler
34	Top	Shutterstock/akturer
35	Top	Wikimedia Commons/Fribbler
36	Bottom	Shutterstock/Rostislav Glinsky
38	Bottom	Wikimedia Commons
40	Top	Shutterstock/William Perugini
42	Top	United Nations Photo/TC
43	Top	Shutterstock/Roman Yunushevsky
44	Bottom	iStock/DJC_Cliff
46	Bottom	Wikimedia Commons/Zorion
48	Top	Wikimedia Commons/Derek Jensen
50	Top	Wikimedia Commons/Southbank Centre
52	Top	Wikimedia Commons/U.S. Department of State
55	Top	Shutterstock/paintings
56	Bottom	iStock/Merijn van der Vliet

Cover	Top	Shutterstock/Everett Historical
Cover	Left	Wikimedia Commons
Cover	Right	Shutterstock/bumihills

About the Author and Advisor

Series Advisor

Ruud van Dijk teaches the history of international relations at the University of Amsterdam, the Netherlands. He studied history at Amsterdam, the University of Kansas, and Ohio University, where he obtained his Ph.D. in 1999. He has also taught at Carnegie Mellon University, Dickinson College, and the University of Wisconsin-Milwaukee, where he also served as editor at the Center for 21st Century Studies. He has published on the East-West conflict over Germany during the Cold War, the controversies over nuclear weapons in the 1970s and 1980s, and on the history of globalization. He is the senior editor of the *Encyclopedia of the Cold War* (2008), produced with MTM Publishing and published by Routledge.

Author

John Perritano is an award-winning journalist, writer, and editor from Southbury, Connecticut, who has written numerous articles and books on a variety of subjects, including history, politics, and culture, for such publishers as Mason Crest, National Geographic, Scholastic, and *Time/Life*. His articles have appeared on Discovery.com, PopularMechanics.com, and other magazines and websites. He holds a master's degree in American History from Western Connecticut State University.